The Scotch-Irish Settlers
in the Valley of Virginia

By Bolivar Christian

Originally published
1860

Our Alma Mater was born of the habitual esteem for learning among the Scotch Irish settlers of this Valley. It had a genial nurture in the classic taste and training of their pastors-hereditary exemplars for their people, not more in piety than in political virtue. Its primal dowry was a tribute from the Father of his country to patriotism and valor, so long and often illustrated under his own eye, from the fatal day of Braddock's defeat till Freedom's crowning conflict on the plains of Yorktown.

The Alumni of Washington College may well find it a fitting duty to trace out, in all its associations, the unwritten history of the Scotch-Irish Settlers in the Valley of Virginia. Of this race most of the Alumni are themselves direct descendants, and dispersed as they now are in every part of this continent, it can be but a labor of love for each to gather as he may, even from the four winds themselves, some Sybilline leaves, or floating traditions, to illustrate a history rich in story of brave men and noble deeds "Sed omnes illachrymabiles; Urgentur, ignotique longâ; Nocte, carent quia vate sacro."

Let us, then, in a spirit of filial love—akin to that of the pious Æneas attempt the task of rescuing from impending oblivion, even so little of the honored memory of our fathers before it be too late forever. Let us as patiently, for the sake of the charity of the undertaking, wander awhile, like Old Mortality, among the graves of the past, and with humble but persistent effort retouch the fading tombstones of virtue.

We propose not to travel along the broad highways of History, but mostly on a more rugged route, amidst remote forests and rude mountains, where only weird Tradition has her trackless haunts. We will attempt not in this brief hour to treat such a theme in artistic style, but only to present, as we have gathered, something of the traits and incidents characteristic of the people and the times in the early days of our Valley, and leave to some more epic pen to trace the moving story in all its fair proportions and poetic contrasts from the simple wigwam homes, the virgin prairies, and forest-covered mountains of this new world, far back to its origin amidst the moors and time-honored highlands of Ancient Scotland, where "Splendor falls on castle walls; And snowy summits old in story."

The familiar term, "Scotch-Irish," implies not the amalgamation of distinct Scotch and Irish families, but like "Anglo-Saxon," and "Indo-Briton," simply that the people of one country were transplanted into the other. The Scotch-Irish Settlers in the Valley of Virginia, are direct descendants of the Scotch who colonized the North of Ireland during the religious troubles of Great Britain, from the reign of Henry VIII., and continuously to the time of William III.

Their lineage is more distinctly traced from the date of the unsuccessful rebellion of the Earls of Tyrconnel and Tyrone, that forfeited to the British crown the factious province of Ulster. Thither James I. transplanted colonies of Scotch and English during the early part of the seventeenth century. The Rev'd Andrew Stewart, a cotemporaneous writer, records, that "of the English not many came over, for it is to be observed that being a great deal more tenderly bred at home in England and entertained in better quarters than they could find in Ireland, they were unwilling to flock

2

thither except to good land, such as they had before at home, or to good cities where they might trade; both of which, in those days, were scarce enough here. Besides, the marshiness and fogginess of this island were still found unwholesome to English bodies. The King, too, had a natural love to have Ireland planted with Scots, as being, besides their loyalty, of a middle temper between the English tender and the Irish rude breeding, and a great deal more likely to adventure to plant Ulster." Among these colonists are mentioned the Ellises, Leslies, Hills, Conways, Wilsons and others, "gentlemen of England and worthy persons" and the Forbeses, Grahams, Stuarts, Hamiltons, Montgomerys, Alexanders, Shaws, Moores, Boyds, Barclays and Baileys, described as "knights and gentlemen of Scotland whose posterity hold good to this day." And here, this evening, I may well repeat this quaint encomium in the presence of many of their lineal posterity, still bearing with honor the same names and "holding good" to this day two full centuries later.

In the channel thus opened the tide of emigration fluctuated from Scotland to Ireland throughout the succeeding century, swollen too long and often from the ruthless persecutions of the unflinching Covenanters by the faithless Charles and his successors, down to the time of the momentous revolution of 1688, which placed the Presbyterian Prince of Orange on the throne of Great Britain.

The history of these people while yet in Scotland, written in the blood of their sufferings, illustrates a character which bore fruit for their descendants in later years and other lands. Under the extraordinary trials and intense excitement of the times exhibiting devotion to their principles of faith and freedom to a degree readily magnified by their enemies, and exaggerated almost to insane fanaticism. Many of them, men of high estate of the nobility of Scotland, sacrificed everything for the common cause, undergoing a persecution which, in the opinion of Bishop Burnet himself, "surpassed even the merciless rigors of the Duke of Alva." Proclaiming, in a loyal petition to a perjured King, that "the only desire of our hearts is for the preservation of true religion amongst us, which we hold far dearer than our lives and fortunes," they resisted to the bitter end the canons and liturgy prepared by the impious Charles without the sanction of any church; driven from their time-honored kirk, they still gathered in conventicles like Maybole, and Ayr, and Remfred, and Teviotdale; renewing, ever and anon, with heartiest zeal, their fealty to their fathers' "SOLEMN LEAGUE and COVENANT," that Magna Charta of Scottish rights, and rallying under their "brave banners," emblazoned at once with the ancient thistle of Scotland and the shibboleth of their own faith in the famous golden letters, "FOR CHRIST'S CROWN AND COVENANT," they awaited, undaunted, the wrath of tyranny defied. Overborne at last by the oppressor's power, goaded by the insolence and cruel tortures of Claverhouse, and Carstairs, Sharpe, Dalzell, and Drummond, too many sealed their testimony with their blood, and the survivors of the red fields of Bothwell-moor, Airsmoss, and Pentland Hills, homeless and hopeless, sought a resting place and refuge amid the fens and bogs of Ulster.

"Ah, days by Scotia still deplored!

When faithless king, and bigot lord,

On their own subjects drew the sword!

"But FIRM in faith of Gospel truth,

Stood hoary age, and guileless youth,

Against oppressors void of ruth,

In cold blood killing wantonly.

"Their preachers silent and deposed,

Their house of prayer against them closed,

Homeless, on mountain heaths exposed!

But though in dark adversity,

Their harps were NOT on willows hung,

But tuneful still, and ever strung,

Till mountain echoes round them rung

To notes of bravest melody!"

They and their descendants, thus saved as by fire, would scarce submit patiently to like oppression in their new-found homes in Ireland. Under the rule of William and Mary, Queen Anne, and the Georges, their condition here was endurable only for its contrast with their former sufferings, the equivocal consolation of the companions of Ulysses "tulimus duriora." Strained constructions of the Act of Toleration; ---tithes and taxes on the wreck of their estates to support an established church, not of their choice; restraints in the exercise of their cherished opinions;

disabilities and degradations to be endured for conscience' sake; peculiar dangers from dwelling amidst such bitter and powerful enemies of their faith, already malignantly gloating over one massacre, and muttering threats for more, all combined to make them an unhappy and restless people.

It was then that like the delusive whisperings of hope in the captive's dream, prophetic tidings came wafting across the wide ocean, that in the far-off forests of America, the Huguenot and Puritan had found a refuge from persecution and "full freedom to worship God." And though the tempest-tossed Eagle-Wing, years before had so trustingly sailed from the same shores only to be driven back a wreck—as their fathers feared and believed by the warning hand of Providence, they yet remembered that the frailer Mayflower, freighted with the hopes of others tried like themselves, had passed over the deep waters in safety. They trusted that now the fullness of time for their departure had come, that the measure of their afflictions in this land was full, and a home in this new world would fulfil, for their relief, the promise of their God, so often hopefully dwelt upon in all their congregations: "For thou O God hast proved us; and thou hast tried us as silver is tried; thou broughtest us into the net, thou layedest affliction upon our loins; thou hast caused men to ride over our heads; we went through fire and through water, BUT THOU BROUGHTEST US OUT UNTO A WEALTHY PLACE."

Gathering what little of worldly gear was left from out of their troubles; many with naught save the Bible, but which alone had so often before, in their sorrowful history, seemed to suffice for even more than spiritual sustenance in many a dreary day, precious as the one draught of sweet water that cheers the patient camel through the weary wastes of the desert, sadly but trustfully they turned away, as they well knew forever, from the homes and the graves of their fathers and fathers' fathers for long centuries gone. Without any known or definite destination within that distant land to which they turned, they hopefully embarked, and in long and wearisome voyages crossing a wide and fathomless ocean that rolled its waves like the dark waters of Lethe over all the crowding memories of their past, they only knew that now their anchors dropped upon the silent shores of another continent, within whose trackless forests they fondly hoped to find at last that peace for body and soul elsewhere so vainly sought. The outcasts of Eden were not more desolate

"Some natural tears they dropt, but wiped them soon;

The world was all before them where to choose

Their place of rest, and Providence their guide."

It was upon the banks of the Delaware they landed, and some rested for a season in the province of Penn, naturally looking for sympathy from a people who in the old world had suffered like themselves for conscience' sake. Others following their native instincts, passed on towards the blue mountains whose towering peaks and waving outlines along the distant horizon recalled the memories of their childhood's home among the hills and heath-clad highlands of Scotland. Ascending the tops of the Kittochtinny, the Indian term for Blue Ridge, they gazed with charmed eye upon this lovely Valley, blooming in all its pristine beauty before them, as on some fairy land they'd longed to see. It fulfilled their fondest dreams of that promised land of peace, as it lay enwrapped in its primal silence, broken only by the sighing of winds among the forest trees, the song of birds, and the sounds of murmuring waters. The long lines of mountain peaks, fading away in distant view, stood ranged on either side like guardian sentinels, while clouds of purple and of gold, gathering along the loftiest crests, hung round the blue horizon like waving banners of welcome.

Tradition relates that the various Indian tribes long held this Valley sacred as a neutral hunting ground. The growth of forest trees was prevented by annual firings at the close of the hunting season, and thus its fertile soil by each returning summer would spread the waving grass over all its plains, and the flowering dogwood, the redbud, azalia, rhododendron, and laurel would crown all its hills with beauty. Lowing herds of buffalo, the stately elk, and the graceful deer in countless numbers found their favourite haunts among the green pastures and beside the still waters of this beautiful vestal land. Like the classic isle of Leuce, it was a modern Elysium, where the forest warriors, elsewhere foes, might here in perfect truce pursue together the pleasures of the chase. Here the wanderers found a genial home, and within a short score of years following their first permanent settlement in 1732, spread along the banks of the Opequon and Cedar creek in the Northern portion of the Valley, and soon over all the waters of the Cohongoruton, and far up its branches to the triple forks of the silvery Sherando. Pressing on Southward and Westward, they settled the sources of the James and Roanoke, the Greenbrier, and the head waters of the Holston.

The government of Virginia with a wise policy encouraged these infant settlements by liberal grants of choice lands, total exemption from taxation for a term of years, and guaranty for freedom in all their forms of religious worship. Thus was secured for the frontier a bold and hardy and loyal people, a palisade of defence in savage warfare, and a proper nursery for pioneers to push her empire Westward to the inviting valley of the Mississippi.

The mountain boundaries of this isolated land stood as obstacles alike to visitors from abroad, and wanderers from their own folds. Settled in clusters of families of the same faith and fatherland, strangers to all others on this side the broad Atlantic, their social desires were satisfied solely within the confines of their own new homes. The luxuriant soil, and abundant game of the forests, afforded in profusion the comforts of their simple life. The pack-horse now and then wending a solitary way across rugged mountains and through trackless forests to the distant cities of Newcastle or to Williamsburg, "when they needed money to pay their quit-rents," measured their commercial intercourse with the outside world.

They could be but a peculiar people. With all the piety, they had none of the ascetic sanctity of the Puritan; with a jealous sense of honour, they had something like the chivalry of the Cavaliers, yet without wealth they escaped the enervating influences of luxury. The common sacrifices of all their fortunes in long contests with the oppressor in their native country left all poor alike, and a common suffering and kindred sympathies subdued all social distinctions. Their untiring struggles for freedom of thought and life, "bequeathed from bleeding sire to son," had brought through succeeding generations a physical and mental training that made them independent in spirit, self-reliant in strength, and "hardy as the Nemean lion's nerve." True types of their ancestral Scottish character, which ever shows to most advantage in adversity, and has been well likened to the sycamore of their native hills, that scorns to be biased in its growth by sun or wind or tempest, but shoots its branches defiantly in every direction, shows no weather-side to the storm, and is broken before it will ever bend.

Religious observance, if not innate, was at least their second nature. Like faithful Abraham, they built the altar wherever they pitched the tent. The Bible mostly furnished their library of faith and of philosophy, enclosing Rouse's version of David's psalms for their poetry. Every tradition extant shows how these sacred words were interwoven like golden threads in all their daily discourse. When the captive survivors of the Carr's Creek massacre, in this (Rockbridge) county, reached the Shawnee towns on the banks of the Muskingum, the Indians in cruel sport called on them to sing. Unappalled by the bloody scenes they had already witnessed, and the fearful tortures awaiting them, within that dark wilderness of forest where all hope of rescue seemed forbidden, undaunted by the fiendish revellings of their savage captors, they sang aloud with the most pious fervor from the 137th Psalm, as they oft had done in more hopeful days within the sacred walls of old "Timber Ridge Church":

"On Babel's streams we sat and wept when Zion we thought on,

In midst thereof we hanged our harps the willow trees among,

For then a song required they who did us captive bring,

Our spoilers called for mirth and said, a song of Zion sing."

From this very familiarity with these sacred psalms, it may well be feared they did not always apply them in such sanctified use as expressions for solace in sorrow; but in the fullness of heart in other emotions, the mouth might well speak these ready words, and naturally enough in the confidential language of faithful love. A lineal descendant tells how his ancestor, when a disconsolate lover because not allowed to visit the lady of his heart from the opposition of her parents, contrived still to interpret his love by the words of the sweet singer of Israel" closing the correspondence" with the stanza from the 63d psalm :

"Oh daughter take good heed, incline and give good ear,

Thou must forget thy kindred all, and father's house most dear,

Thy beauty to the king shall then delightful be,

And do thou humbly worship him, because thy lord is he."

On this hint she acted, and returned to "the king" her answers in kind: On a concerted day the daring lover dashed before the house on a strong charger, and in full view of "brothers and kinsmen and all," like another Lord Lochinvar:

"So light to the croupe the fair lady he swung,

So light to the saddle before her he sprung,

She is won, they are gone, over bank, bush, and scaur,

They'll have fleet steeds to follow that young Lochinvar."

They had constant controversies over doctrines and texts of the Bible. The oldest newspaper extant in Augusta county, contains an advertisement by a lay member of the "Stone Church," appointing a day on which he proposed to discuss his tenets in regard to a certain text, and inviting all who differed in opinion to meet him then and there.

When these men commenced a controversy it was ever most stoutly and persistently maintained; for they were seldom convinced against their will, and if vanquished, would argue still. An old resident of Hay's Creek, in Rockbridge county, contended all his life for his particular theory, as to what tribe of Indians were interred in the mound on that Creek; and on his death-bed made it his most solemn request to be buried on the hill facing the Indian graves, that he might, as he said, be "the first to see the truth of his theory established at the resurrection."

The ministers of the Gospel were true exponents of their people's characteristics. The Rev. John Craig, a Master of Arts of the University of Edinburgh, was for one-third of a century pastor of the "Augusta Church." He walked five miles to service on every Sunday, and in time of the Indian troubles carried a rifle on his shoulder. "Preaching" commenced at 10 o'clock, A. M., and with a recess of one hour at midday, was continued till sunset. One of his sermons, still extant, is divided into fifty-five heads. Walking ever in the example of the upright man of David's psalm, he "spoke truth in the heart," and was "moved not" even in the least thing, from the straightest line of integrity. In choosing the site for a church, the congregation disregarded his opposition, and the "Tinkling Spring" was selected; whereupon he declared that "none of that water should ever 'tinkle' down his throat;" and for thirty years he kept his word, and through his long sermons, in the parching summer days, never once allaying his thirst with a drop from that cool and limpid spring

"For though he promise to his hurt

 He makes his promise good."

Brave and patriotic, after Braddock's disastrous expedition had left the Valley exposed to the raids of the ruthless savages, and the helpless inhabitants in utter consternation were councilling safety in flight, his Journal, yet extant, says, "I opposed that scheme as a scandal to our nation, falling below our brave ancestors, making ourselves a reproach among Virginians, a dishonour to our friends at home, an evidence of cowardice, want of faith, and noble Christian dependence on God, as able to save and deliver from the heathen; and withal a lasting blot forever on all our posterity." He advised the building of forts in convenient places for refuge. His appeal and example had its effect, "for my own flock," he adds, "required me to go before them in the work, which I did cheerfully, though it cost me one-third of my estate; but the people followed, and my congregation, in less than two months, was well fortified." And they maintained their homes most bravely through all the fiery trials of these times. Honoured forever among all their posterity be the name of the noble and pious old patriot! Surviving the subsequent struggles of his adopted country for the freedom he so dearly prized, he fell at last like fruit fully ripe, but mourned by all, and leaving a memory to be revered, and examples of life and faith that like all "the actions of the just; Smell sweet, and blossom in the dust."

Let him be taken as the type and ante-type of the Presbyterian preachers of the Valley, for time will fail to tell of Brown, and Wilson, and Waddell, and Scott, and Graham, and many others; men of thorough learning and approved piety, whose names their descendants should not willingly let die, whose appeals for patriotism will echo in this land while its everlasting hills abide, whose lessons of piety and faith will be effectual for time and for eternity, whose canonized memory will remain among their successors as a monument forever, and stand before them like that lofty "tower which David builded for an armory, whereon there hang a thousand bucklers,— shields of mighty men."

A description of the old covenanters of Scotland, in "Burnett's Own Times," will, in many particulars, singularly illustrate the life of the Scotch-Irish settlers of this Valley, and show an unadulterated descent, and most tenacious maintenance of the customs of their ancestors. Bishop Burnett can scarcely be accused of partiality, and amidst all his charges of affectation, fanaticism and enthusiasm, we may well believe he gives a faithful picture of the old covenanting congregations of his day, by its strong family likeness to the early Presbyterian congregations of this Valley. Of the covenanting ministers ejected by the Glasgow

Act, he writes, "they were a grave and solemn sort of people. Their spirits were eager, and their tempers sour. But they had an appearance that created respect. They used to visit their parishes much; were full of the Scripture, were ready at extempore prayer, and had brought the people to such a degree of knowledge, that cottagers and servants would have prayed extempore. Their ministers brought their people about them on Sunday nights, where the sermon was talked over; and every one, women as well as men, were desired to speak their own experience; and by these means they had a comprehension of matters of religion greater than I have seen among people of that sort anywhere. The preachers went all in one tract, of raising observations on points of doctrine out of their text, and proving these by reasons, and then of applying those, and showing the use that was to be made of such a point of doctrine, both for instruction and terror, for exhortation and comfort, for trial of themselves upon it, and for furnishing them with proper directions and helps. And this was so methodical that the people grew to follow a sermon quite through every branch of it. As they lived in great familiarity with their people, and used to pray and talk oft with them in private, so it can hardly be imagined to what a degree they were loved and reverenced by them. They kept scandalous persons under a severe discipline: for breach of Sabbath, for an oath, or the least disorder in drunkenness, persons were cited before the church session, that consisted of ten or twelve of the chief of the parish, who, with the minister, had this care upon them, and were solemnly reproved for it."

The unexplored records of the courts held for Augusta county, at Staunton, and the church-warden's book for Augusta parish, furnish materials, scanty as they are, that illustrate the lives and characters of this peculiar people. For the purposes of history these records are necessarily insufficient, but give here and there in the technical and curt recitals of court proceedings some incidental cotemporaneous facts which can be confirmed, explained and expanded from other sources; while around them all the mellow light of tradition still falls to impart to these quaint old papers something of the sanctity and value of the illuminated manuscripts of the middle ages.

The court of Orange county had jurisdiction, and its Clerk's office was for a whole decade the depository of the title deeds, and such other papers pertaining to this territory as indispensable necessity required to be recorded. In the year 1738 all Virginia West of the Blue Ridge, was laid off into two counties, called Frederick and Augusta, in honour of the Prince of Wales, and the Princess Augusta. Frederick embraced the Northeastern portion of the Valley, while Augusta extended throughout the West "to the utmost limits of Virginia." The inhabitants were exempted from "all public levies for ten years;" but in 1842, "at the humble suit of the inhabitants of Augusta," an act passed "appointing James Patton, John Christian, and John Buchanan to levy a tax on each tithable, to pay for destroying wolves, relieving the poor, building bridges, and clearing roads" within said county.

The church-warden's book for the Parish of Augusta, commences early in the year 1746. It was doubtless difficult, if not impossible, at that date for the freeholders to find "twelve able and discreet men of the county" from choice "conformable to the doctrine and discipline of the church of England" to serve as their vestry. It is not surprising, therefore, that probably all of the vestry elect were "dissenters," and certainly some of the number who continued as vestrymen for the succeeding quarter of a century, were all the time ruling elders in the Presbyterian churches of Augusta.

In that day of little sectarian excitement between Protestant denominations, it was not so unusual in any part of Virginia to find dissenters take with the oath of secular office a declaration of conformity to the doctrine of the established church, and yet retain their connection with dissenting denominations. The first twelve vestrymen elected by the freeholders of the county in 1745 were all, perhaps, descendants, and some bore the family names of conspicuous Presbyterian covenanters of Scotland; and for over twenty years no notice by the vestry or the Assembly is taken of the fact of their being non-conformists. The usual oaths of conformity were meantime taken, but the vestrymen remaining zealous dissenters. But on the 21st of November, 1767, the following appears on the vestry book: "Ordered, that a minute be taken that the following vestrymen hath subscribed a declaration in Vestry, to be conformable to the doctrine and discipline of the Church of England, according to law, viz: Col. John Buchanan, Mr. Geo. Matthews, Mr. James Lockhart, Mr. John Buchanan, Mr. John Archer, Mr. John Page, and Mr. Wm. Fleming, and enter their dissent against Mr. Israel Christian's signing the proceedings of this Vestry, as he refused signing the declaration in Vestry." The proceedings were signed by all as before, but on the "21st November, 1769 it is ordered that Mr. Thomas Madison be chosen vestryman in room of Capt. Israel Christian, and Capt. Peter Hog in room of Maj. Robt. Breckenridge, the said Breckenridge and Christian having refused subscribing to the doctrine and discipline of the Church of England." (Signed) WM. PRESTON, Clerk of Vestry.

In November, 1769, the Assembly past an Act "dissolving the Vestry of the Parish of Augusta," because "it is represented that a majority of the Vestry are dissenters, &c.," and ordering "an election of twelve new vestrymen." But this Act seems to have been totally disregarded by the "freeholders," the same vestrymen continuing in office long after. The office of vestryman was in effect not a religious one, but simply to discharge the duties of a magistrate of police, of overseers of the poor, to lay the county levies, and to collect fines for "swearing," "drunkenness," and other "foibles," which official duties from the frequency of their "returns," must have occupied no little of their surplus time. The Vestry was finally dissolved during the revolutionary war.

The first court for Augusta county was held at Staunton on the 9th of December, 1745. The magistrates and officers were appointed by the Crown of England, through the Governor of the colony. The court when once organized went to work with a will, and, true to Scotch-Irish instincts, seem to have executed with a special vengeance the Act of Good Queen Anne, "for the effectual suppression of vice, and punishment of wicked blasphemers and dissolute person." This Act seems to have been construed by them as cumulative of the divine decalogue, the "presentments" being made mostly in the order of the offences therein denounced. And the court meted out to unfortunate offenders the full measure of the law, in all its bearings. Some extracts, taken at random through a series of years from the records, will illustrate at once the character of the courts, and of the people.

"May 17th, 1746. The grand-jury, by James Trimble, foreman, made the following presentment," (among others similar:)

"Robert Harper, for being drunk, and swearing 3 prophane oaths."

"Col. Thomas Chew, (a lawyer,) and John Bramham, (deputy sheriff,) as common swearers."

"James as a disturber of the common peace of the neighbours by carrying lies; and also as a common lyer."

"Valentine Sevier, for swearing 6 prophane oaths."

"John Bramham, Bramhan, (deputy Sheriff,) for prophanely desiring God to damn Capt. George Robinson and his company."

"Edward Bogle, for damng the court, and swearing four oaths in their presence," was "put in the stocks for two hours, and fined 20 shillings."

"November 28th, 1750. The Grand Jury presented (among others) Samuel Hutts, for breach of the Sabbath in singing prophane songs."

"James Frame, for a breach of the Sabbath in unnecessarily travelling ten miles."

"Jacob Coger, for breach of the peace by driving hogs over the Blue Ridge on the Sabbath day."

Very many presentments were for "being drunk," and the fines, therefor, averaged about 5 shillings, such appearing to have been about the market price for the privilege. Where the opportunity for the expensive luxury was afforded may be inferred from the following orders of court, establishing rates for ordinary-keepers in 1746, 1747, and 1748:

"Ordered, that the several and respective Ordinary keepers in this county do sell and entertain according to the under-mentioned Rates, and that they presume not to take or demand more of any person whatever—

Father of Gen'l John Sevier, Governor of Tennessee, and of the revolutionary "State of Frankland."

Maderia wine, the quart, "Punch, the quart, with white sugar, three gills of Rum, and so in proportion for a greater or lesser quantity,.... Ditto do with brown sugar, Rum and all cordial spirits, the gallon, Whiskey, the gallon, and so in proportion, (well made,). "Whiskey punch, the quart, with white sugar, do Ditto." "JOHN MADISON, Cl. Curiæ."

The court, after arranging such a bill of fare as the foregoing, could but be lenient on occasion to such as were unwarily led into temptation, and we find the following entry in point:

"May 17th, 1753. Order'd, that ye presentm't ag'st Patrick Shirkey for being drunk be dismissed—the court being of opinion that it was inadvertently done, he being an honest fellow."

Whatever else might be said of this county court, it cannot be alleged they were anywise wanting in the virtue of loyalty, as the following and other like entries on their records will show:

"Feby: 10th, 1746.—The Court being informed that James McClune hath spoke treasonable words, it is ordered that the sheriff bring him before the Court to answer for the same."

"May 17th, 1749. Jacob Castle being accused by the oath of Adam Harman for threatening to goe over to and be aiding and assisting to the French against his Majesty's forces, as appears by precept under the hand of John Buchanan and George Robinson, gentlemen, it's ordered that the sheriff take the said Castle into custody." Father of Bishop Madison.

"Nov. 27th, 1751. The Grand Jury present Owen Crawford for drinking a health to King James (the Pretender) and refusing to drink a health to King George."

"March 17th, 1756. Francis Farguson being brought before the court by warrant under the hand of Robert McClanahan, gent., for damning Robert Dinwiddie, Esqr.," (then Governor of the Colony,) "for a Scotch peddling puppy"-was found guilty, but "excused on apologizing and giving security to keep the peace."

Owen found it good for his own "health" to leave the county before the trial could be held, and the presentment was dismissed subsequently on motion of the King's Attorney.

"March 17th, 1756. Francis Farguson being brought before the court by warrant under the hand of Robert McClanahan, gent., for damning Robert Dinwiddie, Esqr.," (then Governor of the Colony,) "for a Scotch peddling puppy" was found guilty, but "excused on apologizing and giving security to keep the peace."

The Court, moreover, seems to have had as loyal an appreciation of its own dignity, as would appear from more than one order akin to the following concerning one of its "female subjects," who must herself have I been a lineal descendant of the famous Jánet Geddes, of Gray Friar's memory:

"May 17th, 1754. Anne, wife of having come into court, and abused William Wilson, Gent., one of the Justices for this County, by calling him a rogue, and that on his coming off the bench 'she would give it to him with the Devil'-it's ordered that the sheriff take her to the ducking stool."

"May 17th, 1754. Anne, wife of having come into court, and abused William Wilson, Gent., one of the Justices for this County, by calling him a rogue, and that on his coming off the bench 'she would give it to him with the Devil,' it's ordered that the sheriff take her to the ducking stool."

This imposing Court had jurisdiction over a territory comprising all the counties of Western Virginia, (except Frederick,) and also what now constitutes adjoining States; its jail was filled with offenders from as far as the city of Pittsburg, now in Pennsylvania. The court usually met at 7 o'clock in the morning and sat till night. As curiosity may well exist to know something of the state in which these dignitaries of the British Crown were accustomed to sit, it may fortunately be gratified by the following extract from one of its Grand Jury presentments:

"At a court con'd and held for Augusta county, May 21st, 1748.

"The grand jury made the following presentment:

"We have viewed and Examined this Court-house and prison, and find the court-house to be thirty-eight feet three inches long, and eighteen feet three inches wide in the clear, built with logs hewed on both sides, not laid close, some of the cracks between the logs quite open, four or five inches wide and four or five feet long, and some stopped with chunks and clay, but not one quite close: two small holes cut for windows, but no glass nor shutters to them; the inside not finished nor fitting for his Majesty's Judicature to sit. The Jury Rooms too small and not furnished with tables, benches, &c., fitting for a grand and petty jury to sit; and no part of it finished as it ought to be, excepting only the roof, which was lately repaired.

"The prison to be twenty-two feet three inches long, and seventeen feet three inches wide, from out-side to outside, built with square logs near one foot thick, holes at ye corners and elsewhere two or three inches wide, and so poorly dove-tailed at the corners, that it would be a very easy matter to pull it all down. The chymney that was formerly built in a very poor manner, now part of it is down, so that there is an open way to the roof which a man might easily break with his foot or hands.

"For which reasons we present them."

"WM. CHRISTIAN, foreman."

Although George Wythe, the Pendletons and others "qualified and took their places at the bar," as lawyers, some as early as 1747, they do not appear to have been regular practitioners; and the people seem to have been at more inconvenience for lawyers then than is now the case at the Staunton bar, as would appear from the following order of court:

"August 28th, 1751. On petition of Andrew Bird, &c., that James Porteus in his lifetime brought suit for him against Peter Scholl, and that said Scholl hath imployed Gabriel Jones and John Harvie, Gents., the only attornies that attend this bar, and praying that one of said attornies be assigned him. Ordered that John Harvie, Gent., be assigned," &c.

An order of court was entered as early as February 12th, 1746, which does not appear from the records to have ever been rescinded, and the court at the present day might find it profitable, as a source of revenue at least, and of consternation to the bar, to enforce. It is to be hoped the necessity for such an order is no greater now than it should have been then with their only two attorneys.

"February 12th, 1746. Ordered that any attorney interrupting another at the bar, or speaking when he is not employed, forfeit five shillings."

Gabriel Jones was the first, and for years the only lawyer residing in the county. He lived near the present town of Port Republic, (in Rockingham county,) and the road he travelled to court was opened, in 1746, by an order for "laying off a road from the clerk's office" (long kept at Port

Republic) "to the court-house," and is still known as "the lawyer's road." His influence with the court was naturally great, and he was justly regarded as indispensable. It is a current tradition that the late Judge Holmes, when a young man, mischievous and witty, once as opposing counsel provoked Mr. Jones into such a furious passion that he became very profane. The court consulted long as to what should be done; to punish "Squire Jones" was out of the question, but the dignity of the bench and the majesty of the law had to be preserved, and finally the presiding justice pronounced as the decision of the court, "That if Mr. Holmes did not quit worrying Mr. Jones, and making him swear so profanely, then Mr. Holmes should be sent to jail."

The county levies, as laid by the courts, are also suggestive of historic incidents:

On the 20th November, 1746, the levy was laid on 961 tithables, at "34 pounds of tobacco, or 2 shillings and 1 penny per poll." In 1747 the levy was on 1670; in 1750 on 2122; in 1752 on 2317 tithables.

The usual subjects of county expense were "premiums on wolves' heads," "salary of the deputy attorney of the king,"—(Gabriel Jones)—"Burgesses' wages,"—(James Patton)—and the following as a standing item, viz: "To Robert McClenahan to find small beer; candles; to keep the court-house in order; to find stabledge for Justices', attornies', and officers' horses, 1600 pounds of tobacco."

In a levy made November 19th, 1755, are the following items:

"To John Harrison for burying some Robbers by him killed; and for expenses to Dr. Lynn for dressing the wounds of one of them, 640 pounds.

"To John Harrison for going for a coroner, and other expenses about the above mentioned Robbers, 310 pounds of tobacco."

Making about $10 in money for the complete job and no further notice appears on the records concerning this killing of "some Robbers." But at a court held previously, viz: February 19th, 1751, is this entry, "The petition of John and Reuben Harrison, praying a reward for killing two persons under the command of Utes Perkins, who were endeavouring to rob them, was read and ordered to be certified."

From these, and other frequent entries concerning "Utes Perkins and his followers," it is obvious, that during several years about that date there was an organized band of robbers within the then limits of Augusta county. It is not known that any tradition is extant concerning the matter. In 1744 an Act of Assembly was passed, "to punish horse-stealing, and receivers of stolen cattle and horses," and recites in one section that "the crime of horse-stealing is of late years much increased, especially in the frontier counties of this colony," &c., &c. This has reference doubtless to Augusta, and it is probable that "Perkins and his company" were principally horse thieves, as entries show that they generally appeared with horses in possession.

The sheriffs' returns upon unsatisfied executions were likewise illustrative of the times. Discarding such classic technicalities of the profession as "Nulla bona," and "non est inventus," and the like, they adopted a more practical and pointed style. A few specimens must suffice:

"August 15th, 1749. Our Sovereign Lord the King vs. Sam'l Stalnaker, ca. sa.—Not executed by reason of badness of the weather and freshets.

"RO. BRECKINRIDGE, D. S." "Elliott vs. Johnson, Not executed by reason of the flux being in the house.

"RO. BRECKINRIDGE, D. S." "Nov'r, 1752.— Williams vs. Bulger.—Not executed by reason of an axe.

"JOHN LEWIS, D.S." 6 May, 1753.—Williams vs. Bulger.—Not executed by reason of a gun.

"J. LEWIS, D. S." "Nov'r, 1756.—Not executed by reason the defendant outrode me, so that I could not catch him.

"SAMPSON Matthews. D. S." "Feb'y, 1758."—Very many returns are made. "Not executed by reason the river is not rideable.

"WM. BOWYER, D. S." "Feb'y 1763. Reed vs. Clendening. Not executed by reason the fellow gave me heel play.

"GEORGE SKILLERN, D. S." "Nov'r, 1762. Young vs. Greer. Not ex'd. Issue this against cousin again, and perhaps after next court we may have better luck.

"G. SKILLERN, D. S."

But the "luck" seems to have remained with "cousin" throughout, judging by the following returns in the same case:

"Feb'y, 1763.—This is my friend's—issue it again, and I shall storm his castle once more.

"GEO. SKILLERN, D. S."

"June, 1763. Issue this against the body once more, and I will lie at his house all night but I will have him.

"GEO. SKILLERN, D. S."

The sheriffs were also evidently disposed to exercise equity powers "on horseback" in those days, as the following returns would indicate:

"Schall vs. Miller.—Executed, but it is wrong.

Mr. Jones can inform WM. LUSK, D. S."

"Dec'r 22d, 1756.—Ramsay vs. Burton. Not executed by reason the defendant produced his receipt from Israel Christian, Gent., for £30, on account of a judgment obtained by said Christian and John Ramsay against the deft.; and R. W. Renix informed me that he was by when Christy gave the receipt, and Ramsay at the same time, who was agreed to put a stop to the suit against Burton, and that there should be no further proceedings on it. SAMPSON MATTHEWS, Sh'ff."

But this "interlocutory decree" seems to have been unavailing, as there was the following subsequent return in the same case at that term, which ought to have been as satisfactory as the plea in the "cracked kettle case."

"Ramsay vs. Burton. Not executed by stress of water, and deft. swore if I did get over to him, he would shoot me if I touched any of his estate; also he is gone out of the county.

"SAMPSON MATTHEWS, Sh'ff."

From 1755 to 1759, the years immediately succeeding Braddock's direful defeat—and thence almost continuously to "Dunmore's war" in 1774—very many returns were substantially like the following, and indicative of the dangers of the times:

"Nov'r, 1756. Not executed by reason the way was dangerous for Indians. S. MATTHEWS, Sh'ff."

"Feb'y 1758. Not executed by reason of the enemy Indians ranging so that I can't get up where the defendant lives.

"WM. BOWYER, D. S."

"March 28th, 1758. Not executed by reason of the heathen Indians ranging so that I can't get up there.

"WM. BOWYER, D. S."

But these record books disclose for the history of this people a page of far more serious import. Brief cotemporaneous entries on many a leaf indicate the date of the dreaded Indian incursions into this valley and mark the places of the bloody massacres remembered long with mourning among their descendants to the third and fourth generation. Names of men, and captains of companies, in numbers that will surprise their posterity of to-day, appear on these pages, through the long period of thirty years, with short intervals of uncertain peace, as actively engaged in aggressive and defensive war with their wily and relentless forest foes.

Stretched along the frontiers, separated by mountains and by miles of forests from the seat of their colonial government, whence only succor could be claimed; poorly provided with means of defense, they were left in their own unaided strength exposed to all the troubles engendered by the long and bitter contest between the French and English nations for supremacy in the West. But they bore the brunt most bravely, and stood, withal, a sure rock of defense to dash back the merciless wave of savage warfare from the hearth-stones of the East.

"Expeditions," composed of hundreds of men, appear from these records to have "gone out as rangers on the frontiers," at periods of which history makes no other mention than in the few unnoticed acts of the assembly, which acknowledge and encourage such services. Companies of "Rangers," "Independents," and "Volunteers," under such captains as the Lewises, McClenahans, Cunninghams, Prestons, Dickinsons, Dunlaps, Alexanders, and others, armed with their own rifles, and equipped at their own expense, penetrated the dark forest in all directions, to punish and disperse the marauding parties of savages, who, for real or fancied wrongs, in times otherwise of peace, with scalping-knife and torch fell upon defenceless families to murder and destroy, and again disappear as stealthily as the panther and wolf to their distant lairs.

Thinly settled as was Augusta in 1754, a company, under Captain Lewis, was sent to join the youthful Washington in his first battle at the Great Meadows. In Braddock's ill-starred defeat, in 1755, the "backwoods riflemen of Augusta, under the eye of Washington, were most effective in staying the sad fortunes of that fatal day. In 1757, at the call of the Government, a most formidable force marched from the county to invade the distant country of the Shawnese, and had already reached the Ohio, when, to their great chagrin, they were recalled by the colonial governor, and had to retrace their perilous route for hundreds of miles through a deep snow and a mountain wilderness, their provisions exhausted, and dependent for food only on the game and the wild nuts of the forest, and finally on the flesh of their pack-horses and the leather of their rude saddles; but the skill and intrepidity of their able commander, Andrew Lewis, led them to their homes at last, but worn-out with fatigue and starvation. And again, in 1758, a battalion of these hardy riflemen, under their favorite leader, marched to the distant banks of the Ohio, and, hearing the firing at the battle of "Grant's hill," they pressed on contrary to orders, and reached the field in time to save the defeated Highlanders from inevitable slaughter. In 1760, in Colonel Bouquet's successful expedition to the Muskingum towns, and all throughout Pontiac's long war, and afterwards against the Cherokees of the South, company after company went from Augusta. And on the 10th of October, 1774, the bloody drama was at last closed in the utter rout of the Indian forces, in a pitched battle, fought hand to hand, "from morn to noon, from noon to dewy eve," by over one thousand on either side, of these hardy forest warriors, on the ever memorable field of Point Pleasant.

The individual distress that attended such times as these may well be yet remembered with horror. The families and firesides of these frontier soldiers on their long expeditions were necessarily left almost defenceless. In the single summer of 1758 as many as sixty persons in the county of Augusta were massacred in their homes. Their fields were uncultivated, and whole settlements were often reduced almost to famine, but still they fought on bravely, with a patriotic devotion of the best years of their lifetime to their country. It was doubtless true of many, as tradition yet tells of Charles Lewis, that very flower of forest chivalry, who fell so untimely while leading the van at Point Pleasant, that during the Indian wars, for ten long years, he was not permitted to remain as much as a month at any one time with his family and his home.

Though history has no sufficient record of these frontier wars, it must not be inferred they were any the less formidable. So far away in the uninhabited forests, the ear of history could scarce catch the sound of the battles, and no earthly eye was witness, save that of the wheeling vulture and hungry wolf, awaiting the expected prey. They were fought only in the direst necessity for fighting, amidst nothing but its horrors, against savage foes, a fierce, unrelenting struggle for very life and death, with no hope for relief or respite in the bitter strife, until only the king of terrors should decide; fought, too, all without the accustomed incentives of other battlefields, nor cheered by fame's prophetic voice, nor "glory's thrill," which, more than trumpet's blast, stirs the blood to chivalrous deeds, elevates war awhile above its cruelties, almost "makes ambition virtue," and inspires the soul with that true heroism to brave "the perilous hour; Whatever the shape in which death may lower; For FAME is there to tell who bleeds; And HONOR's eye marks daring deeds."

But there is no need to dwell on the horrors of such warfare. The term Indian, so euphonious in itself has become a synonym with savage. The thrilling tales of these fearful times, told in every nursery throughout this valley, awaken the earliest fears of our infancy, and "run moulten still in memory's mould." There is more danger that the inflamed imagination may do an injustice at once to the Indian and the white warrior, and to the character of the contest itself. The Indian, though savage, was not a wild beast, and mercy and humanity could not be altogether disregarded; nor must the dire scenes enacted be tried by the rules of civil warfare. Much might be told to extenuate, if not atone for, the cruelties committed; much of provocation to these free-born spirits of the forest; much to inflame their native thirst for vengeance, and but too many deeds of indiscriminate murder, like that which fired the forest-born eloquence of Logan-the Mingo chief to tell his wrongs to all coming times, "in thoughts that breathe and words that burn." The untutored Indian, in his rude forest life, devoid of all motives to soften or conceal his passions, displays but the common weakness of man's nature in colors the more vivid only because on simpler ground. Nemesis, the Goddess of Vengeance, has her votaries in every age and every clime.

Imagination may too well supply the horrors of this savage warfare, and it would be a more gracious task, if time permitted, to relieve the dark shades of the picture, and farther illustrate the story with some of the many traditions that show these warriors of nature were not to be despised either as friends or as foes. If savage life had vices, it was not all devoid of virtues. Their history is full of touching incidents of magnanimity, from the romantic tenderness of Pocahontas in shielding the adventurous Smith from the war-clubs of Powhatan, down to the times and the homelier tales of generous deeds towards the settlers of this valley. If we shudder at their brutal sport in making their captives "run the gauntlet," we can but smile withal over the story of young Schoolcraft, who, on receiving the first blow as he entered the "gauntlet," turned lustily to fight the Indian who struck him, when all the others at once left the lines, crowded round the boy, and encouraged him in the contest, until he conquered the Indian; and forthwith he was released, to become a privileged favorite in the tribe. At the bloody massacre on Carr's Creek, in Rockbridge county, an Indian, while scalping Thomas Gilmore, was knocked down by Mrs. Gilmore with an iron kettle; another Indian ran with uplifted tomahawk to kill her, and was only stopped by the one who lay bleeding from the blow she had given him, calling quickly to him, "don't kill her, she is a good warrior;" and this magnanimity in a savage saved her life.

Tradition in the Trimble family of Augusta tells that the beautiful farm yet in their possession was shown their ancestor by an Indian, in return for some favor done him long before in the woods of Pennsylvania, and that for many years afterwards, when the Indians appeared in this neighborhood for murder and rapine, that family was always unmolested, though visited, and a draught of fresh milk from the dairy and a mess of hominy invariably demanded and taken, as a token of peace. The families of

Bumgarner, Croft, and some others, obtained by, treaty from the Indians, permission to settle and hunt upon the Monongahela river; but when the war of 1774 commenced, Governor Dunmore sent a message to warn them that if they remained all would be killed. An Indian who happened to hear it delivered, replied most indignantly to the messenger, "tell your king he is damned liar; Indian no kill these men." And the families in fact remained there unharmed throughout all the horrors of that bloody war.

So comparatively silent is history concerning this border warfare, that few appreciate how formidable were the Indian warriors in battle. Their personal daring, ferocity, and untiring thirst for revenge may be known, but they are regarded still as ignorant savages, unskilled to conduct campaigns, and contend in associated armies against the trained troops of civilized life. The fallacy of this idea could be readily shown, but it must suffice here to glance only at the characteristics of the principal chieftains that led them in these wars, and whose devotion to the interests of their people, wisdom in council, skill in strategy and chivalric boldness in battle, have left a fame and "a name to other times" that may well rival the glory of the proudest heroes of the world.

The "great Emperor Pontiac," the war-chief of the Ottowas, the most influential of the Northern tribes, was the first who appeared in the hostile field against the settlers of this valley. He was described by one writer who knew him, as "a person of remarkable appearance, of singularly fine countenance, and of commanding stature." Another says he "habitually wore an air of princely grandeur;" and "the many acts of magnanimity which illustrated his life might have made him a fit comrade for the knights of the middle ages." Another adds, that "in point of native talent, courage, magnanimity, and integrity, he will compare without prejudice with the most renowned of civilized potentates and conquerors."

He first appears in history, in 1746, as the leader of the Indian forces that successfully defended the French in Detroit against an attack of hostile tribes. In the Acadian wars, in 1747, he fought with the French, as the leader of the Indian allies, against the English, and he was the most conspicuous chieftain in the defence of Fort Duquesne. And on that ever memorable morning of the 9th July, 1755, when the crystal waters of the Monongahela glittered with the sheen of burnished arms and brilliant uniforms of the British troops, under the brave but boastful Braddock, all unconscious that the silent forests covered with its shadows a host of hidden foes, it was Pontiac who devised that fatal ambuscade, and headed the allied bands of Indians and French that rushed down on the devoted army, "like the wolf on the fold," left eight hundred men lifeless on that field of blood, and drove the survivors back in utter affright to Fort Cumberland, "the farthest flight," says Smollet, "that any army ever made."

The war of 1763, known in history as "Pontiac's war," was one of the most comprehensive ever conceived in all the annals of Indian warfare, and fell with its greatest fury on the settlements of the Valley, and throughout the West. Pontiac visited in person most of the Northern nations, and his influence was felt from the Mizpacs of Nova Scotia to the

Cherokees of the South. More than twenty tribes assembled at his call in the council of Niagara, where his wonderful natural eloquence, through winning appeals to the pride and even the superstitions of the Indian warriors, soon enlisted all enthusiastically in his as a common cause.

Pontiac, himself, planned the entire campaign, assigning the time, the tribe, and the war-chief to attack each one of the English posts on the extended frontier from Canada to Carolina. It was most promptly put in execution: nine British forts were surprised and captured in rapid succession, the trading posts were all destroyed, and the captives murdered. The forts which withstood the assault were beleaguered for weary months by hostile savages without, and appalled by gaunt famine within. Marauding parties pushed far into the panic-stricken settlements, and committed the memorable massacres of Muddy Creek and the Big Levels on the Greenbrier and Roanoke, in Virginia, and in one merciless slaughter depopulated the whole Valley of Wyoming, in Pennsylvania.

This daring and determined war of the red men of the wilderness called forth the utmost strength of the colonies, and the strongest support of the mother country to conquer it. Finally, General Broadstreet's successful foray quelled the savages of the North; and in the South, the brave and skilful Colonel Bouquet, in command of the provincial troops, among whom were many companies from the county of Augusta, pushed far into the Indian country on the Muskingum and Ohio, and compelled the savages to sue for peace. But Pontiac, scorning to come to any terms, retired to the tribes of Illinois, and while engaged in rallying another general movement, was assassinated by a traitor Indian, whose whole tribe was afterwards totally exterminated by the Ottawas, in revenge for the death of their great chieftain. A distinguished writer says that "the memory of the great Ottowa chief is yet held in reverence among the Indians of the West, and whatever the fate which may await them, his name and deeds will live in their traditionary narratives, increasing in interest as they increase in years."

The peace which ensued the death of Pontiac was, to the frontier settlers, one in name only. Too many bitter memories of the bloody war, just closed, rankled in the savage breasts to allow the fell spirit of revenge so suddenly to submit at the command for peace. The beautiful "Indian Summer," when the brilliant hues of autumnal leaves robe the mountains as with the very banners of peace, was the leisure season of the Indian, and the hereditary time for his annual hunting carnival in these valleys. Such, too, was the fatal time selected for incursions by predatory parties of Indians, year after year, and their path was so often marked by murder and rapine, that the whites were provoked to as fierce retaliations, until finally another "Indian war" blazed out along all the borders of Virginia.

The Shawnese war-chief, Cornstalk, in youth a follower of Pontiac, was the principal leader in this later war, and may be taken as the type of the other chieftains, only less distinguished, but whom time will not permit us to mention. In the sphere for which he was designed, Cornstalk was one of Nature's masterpieces—a consistent advocate of peace, but a thunderbolt in war, bravest in action, most sagacious in camp, and most eloquent in council. The Shawnese, of whom Cornstalk was emperor, "held all other men, Indians as well as whites, in contempt as warriors in comparison with themselves, and were assuming and imperious in the presence of all others not of their nation." Cornstalk was their fitting type and chieftain. He is described as "distinguished for beauty of person, for agility and strength of 'frame, in manners graceful and easy, and in movement majestic and princely."

The famous battle of Point Pleasant, so mournfully familiar to the memory of the descendants of those engaged in it, was the most noted pitched battle ever fought with the Indians upon this continent. Cornstalk commanded the Indian force, which was composed of over one thousand picked warriors, the flower of their tribes. The time and the ground for the battle was selected by Cornstalk with the most consummate sagacity. He designed to cut off by surprise the army of General Lewis, while wornout with the fatigue of its long march through the mountain wilderness, before the approaching reinforcement under Colonel Christian could arrive, and before it could form a junction with the main body of Virginians under Lord Dunmore, who was marching leisurely along the open road of Braddock's expedition. The battle was begun at early dawn, and was most fiercely fought until the sun sank behind the western hills. An actor in the scene says, "the long lines of the opposing armies, stretching for a mile between the banks of the Kanawha and the Ohio, were often within twenty feet of each other, and for a time the fight was hand to hand with tomahawk and war-club and knife, in deadly struggle." The towering form of Cornstalk was constantly seen passing rapidly along the Indian lines, and his clear commanding voice was distinctly heard above the din of battle, cheering his braves with his battle-cry, "BE STRONG! BE STRONG!" One of his warriors appearing to falter, the stern chief, with a blow of his own tomahawk, was seen to cleave the coward's skull. Nothing but the obstinate bravery, and desperate courage of Andrew Lewis, and his experienced officers and hardy men, could have withstood this fierce onslaught; but their unflinching valor triumphed, and the confident Indian was driven back across the Ohio, never again to appear in battle array on the unconquered soil of Virginia.

In the conferences for peace which followed this battle, he extorted the highest praises from the English officers for his remarkable eloquence. "When Cornstalk rose to reply to Lord Dunmore," says Colonel Wilson, (a British officer present,) "he was in no wise confused or daunted, but spoke in a distinct and audible voice, without stammering or repetition, and with peculiar emphasis. His very looks, while addressing Dunmore, were truly grand, yet graceful and attractive." As he advanced and became excited his voice rose in swelling cadence until he could be distinctly heard over all the camp-ground. Colonel Wilson adds, "I have heard the first orators in Virginia-Patrick Henry and Richard Henry Lee-but never have I heard one whose powers of delivery surpassed those of Cornstalk."

The well known story of his death, which occurred but a few years later, so little to the credit of those concerned, was but characteristic of the chieftain himself. Faithfully regarding the treaty of peace, he visited the fort at Point Pleasant to warn the garrison of the efforts of British agents to incite the Indians to take up arms against the Virginians in the revolutionary war. But Cornstalk was detained as a hostage, and his son, the young chief Ellinipsico, in filial devotion, came to the fort to share his father's confinement. A reckless party of soldiers, infuriated at the murder of a comrade by a prowling Indian, alleged to have been a companion of Ellinipsico, rushed to avenge themselves on the helpless hostages. Cornstalk seeing their approach, and having on that same morning expressed a presentiment of approaching death, readily divined their object, and after saying encouragingly to Ellinipsico, "My son, the Great Spirit has seen fit that we should die together, and has sent you here to that end, it is his will, let us submit, it is all for the best," he turned, undauntedly, to meet his murderers, and baring his bosom, received seven balls in his body and fell lifeless at their feet. He was the last of a long line of forest warriors since the days of Powhatan, who, on Virginia's soil, had illustrated, amidst all their cruelties, the loftiest virtues of Nature's heroes; with him departed the spirit and prestige of Indian power forever on this frontier, and the long and bloody drama was fittingly closed with the scene of his death, as he lay thus on the very field of his fame and his greatest battle:—"the lord of all; The forest heroes; trained to wars; Quivered and plumed; and lithe and tall, And seamed with glorious scars."

With such an eventful close of the border hostilities the settlers of this valley might well hope to repose calmly at last in the sun-light of peace; but the luried flashes of these forest wars had scarce faded behind the hills of the West, when their Eastern skies grew dark along all the horizon with the gathering clouds of the revolutionary contest for their country's freedom. But here the headlands of history come into view, and in accordance with the plan of this address, to trespass little on such well known ground, we but linger awhile where we may yet gather some floating traditions, or less known incidents, that farther exhibit the traits of this Scotch-Irish race.

Though wearied and wasted by their long conflicts with their forest foes, and welcome as rest might well have been, still they greeted the coming struggle most cheerily, although against the mother country and the most imperious power of the old world, since it became necessary to secure the rights of conscience and of liberty, which they and their fathers had so long and ever so unceasingly sought. To show the spirit, still worthy of their descent, in which they ripened for the coming revolution, we need but quote, so far as space permits, from the "addresses" of their public meetings of the day, not published as yet in any formal book of history. Augusta was, by this date, sub-divided into the counties of Botetourt and Fincastle, and they who moved in these meetings were the same men, and their immediate descendants, who came from the heart of original Augusta, that "officina gentium" for the West.

On the 20th of January, 1775, months before the famous "Mecklenburg Declaration of Independence," itself the work of the Scotch-Irish of North Carolina, the freeholders of Fincastle, through their committee, consisting of Colonel William Christian, as chairman, Rev'd Charles Cumings, Colonel William Preston, Captain Stephen Trigg, Major Arthur Campbell, Major William Ingliss, Captains Walter Crockett, John Montgomery, James M. Gavock, William Campbell, Thomas Madison, Daniel Smith, William Russell, Evan Shelby and William Edmundson, presented an address to the Continental Congress containing these sentiments:

"Had it not been for our remote situation, and the Indian War in which we were lately engaged to chastise these cruel and savage people for the many murders and depredations they committed amongst us, now happily terminated, we should, before this time, have made known our thankfulness for the very important services you have rendered your country.

"We assure you, and all our countrymen, that we are a people whose hearts overflow with love and duty to our lawful Sovereign George III., whose illustrious House, for several successive reigns, have been the Guardian, of the civil and religious rights and liberties of British subjects as settled at the glorious Revolution; that we are willing to risk our lives in the service of His Majesty for the support of the Protestant Religion, and the rights and liberties of his subjects, as they have been established by Compact, Law and Ancient Charters. We are heartily grieved at the differences which now subsist between the parent State and the Colonies, and most ardently wish to see harmony restored on an equitable basis, and by the most lenient measures that can be devised by the heart of man. Many of us and our forefathers left our native land, considering it as a Kingdom subjected to inordinate power, and greatly abridged of its liberties; we crossed the Atlantic and explored this then uncultivated wilderness, bordering on many nations of Savages, and surrounded by Mountains almost inaccessible to any but those very Savages, who have incessantly been committing barbarities and depredations on us since our first seating the country. These fatigues and dangers we patiently encountered, supported by the pleasing hope of enjoying those rights and liberties which had been granted to Virginians, and were denied us in our native country, and of transmitting them inviolate to our posterity; but even to these remote regions the hand of unlimited and unconstitutional power hath pursued us to strip us of that liberty and property, with which God, nature and the rights of humanity have vested us. We are ready and willing to contribute all in our power for the support of His Majesty's Government, if applied to constitutionally, and when the grants are made to our Representatives, but cannot think of submitting our liberty or property to the power of a venal British Parliament, or to the will of a corrupt British Ministry. We by no means desire to shake off our duty or allegiance to our lawful Sovereign, but on the contrary, shall ever glory in being the loyal subjects of a Protestant Prince, descended from such illustrious progenitors, so long as we can enjoy the free exercise of our Religion as Protestants, and our Liberties and Properties as British Subjects.

"But, if no pacific measures shall be proposed or adopted by Great Britain, and our enemies will attempt to dragoon us out of those inestimable privileges, which we are entitled to as subjects, and to reduce us to slavery, we declare that we are deliberately and resolutely determined never to surrender them to any power upon earth but at the expense of our lives.

"These are our real, though unpolished sentiments, of liberty and loyalty, and in them we are resolved to live and die." (Am. Archives, 1775.)

The Freeholders of Augusta county assembled in Staunton on the 22nd day of February, 1775, chose MR. THOMAS LEWIS and CAPT SAM'L MCDOWELL as delegates to represent them in Colony Convention at the town of Richmond, on the 20th day of March, 1775. "Instructions" were drawn up by Rev. Alex. Balmain, Sampson Matthews, Capt. Alexander McClenachan, Michael Bowyer, Wm. Lewis, and Capt. George Matthews, portions of which are as follows:

"To Mr. Thomas Lewis and Capt. Sam'l McDowell:

"The Commissioners of Augusta county, pursuant to the trust reposed in them by the Freeholders of the same, have chosen you to represent them in a Colony Convention, proposed to be held in Richmond on the 20th March, instant. They desire that you may consider the people of Augusta county as impressed with just sentiments of loyalty and allegiance to his Majesty, King George, whose title to the Imperial Crown of Great Britain rests on no other foundation than the liberty, and whose glory is inseparable from the happiness of all his subjects. We have also a respect for the parent state, which respect is founded on religion, on law, and the genuine principles of the Constitution. On these principles do we earnestly desire to see harmony and a good understanding restored between Great Britain and America. Many of us and our forefathers left our native land, and explored this once savage wilderness, to enjoy the free exercise of the rights of conscience and of human nature. These rights we are fully resolved, with our lives and fortunes, inviolably to preserve; nor will we surrender such inestimable blessings, the purchase of toil and danger, to any Ministry, to any Parliament, or any body of men upon earth, by whom we are not represented, and in whose decisions therefore we have no voice. * * And as we are determined to maintain unimpaired that liberty which is the gift of Heaven to the subject of Britain's Empire, we will most cordially join our countrymen in such measures, as may be deemed wise and necessary to secure and perpetuate the ancient, just, and legal rights of this Colony and all British America.

"As the state of this Colony greatly demands that Manufactures should be encouraged by every possible means, we desire that you use your endeavors that Bounties may be proposed by the Convention for the making of Salt, Steel, Wool-Cards, Paper and Gun-Powder; and that, in the meantime, a supply of Ammunition be provided for the Militia of this Colony. A well regulated Militia is the natural strength and security of a free government, and we therefore wish it recommended by the Convention to the officers and men of each county in Virginia to make themselves masters of the military exercise, published by order of his Majesty in the year 1764.

"Placing our ultimate trust on the Supreme Disposer of every event, without whose gracious interposition the wisest schemes may fail of success, we desire you to move the Convention that some day, which may appear to them most convenient, be set apart for imploring the blessing of ALMIGHTY GOD on such plans as human wisdom and integrity may think necessary to adopt for preserving America, happy, virtuous and free."

The address of the Freeholders of Botetourt, about the same date, is very similar in sentiment and construction with the foregoing, and concludes as follows: "In these sentiments we are determined to live and die. We are too sensible of the inestimable privileges enjoyed by subjects under the British Constitution, even to wish for a change, while the free enjoyments of those blessings can be secured to us; but, on the contrary, can justly boast of our loyalty and affection to our most gracious Sovereigns, and of our readiness in risking our lives, whenever it has been found necessary, for the defence of his person and government.

"But, should a wicked and tyrannical Ministry, under the sanction of a venal and corrupt Parliament, persist in acts of injustice and violence towards us, they only must be answerable for the consequences. Liberty is so strongly impressed on our hearts, that we cannot think of parting with it but with our lives. Our duty to GOD, OUR COUNTRY, OURSELVES, AND OUR POSTERITY, all forbid it. We therefore stand prepared for every contingency."

These addresses have the ring of the true metal; and they display a spirit still living in these people that proved an unadulterated descent from their patriot ancestors of the past. The same independence in thought, resolute maintenance of right, and loyalty to a just government; but an ever-jealous vigilance of tyranny, bold defiance of unrighteous power, prompt resistance of all encroachments on liberty and conscience, and still crowning all a constancy in faith and deep reverence for religion to shed a golden glow over all their daily deeds.

It is believed that, in point of time, the very first paper presented to the continental Congress, distinctly proposing a separation from the government of Great Britain, was one from this people of Augusta: but, unfortunately, the paper itself cannot now be found. The very early date of the addresses quoted, prepared by a people so remote from the commercial and social heart of the colonies, as to be the last to feel the practical evils of oppression, proves not merely the promptness with which they made and met the issue, but that the impulse with them was one of PRINCIPLE alone. And such glowing evidence of sympathy from the distant backwoods might well send an electric thrill through the breast of every patriot in their common country, uniting all in a common cause, with a common pledge to each other of their lives, their fortunes and their sacred honor.

From apprehensions too well justified by bitter experience in the past, that the treacherous Indian might forego his treaty of peace, and again fall upon a defenceless frontier, few troops were taken from the Valley in the early part of the Revolution: but, singly, many joined the army; and although losing their identity as a class, became distinguished as soldiers and officers- the Lewises, Matthews, Campbells and others, in the highest ranks, skilled by long service in the border wars, winning imperishable renown in their country's history.

On the fields of the Cowpens and Guilford some organized companies from the Valley of Virginia were engaged, and bore the brunt of the battle like veterans. Armed each with his own trusty rifle, and skilled in its use from earliest boyhood; familiar with the most perilous forms of warfare from experience with their savage foes; inspired by patriotic zeal in their cause, and brave by very nature, even if undisciplined, they must still have been most effective troops. Some British prisoners asked, after the battle of Guilford, to be shown one of the guns used by these companies, and viewing it with intensest interest exclaimed, that "God and law should forbid the use of such deadly weapons." The Rev. Samuel Houston, a private in the Rockbridge company, "admits" in his Journal, yet extant, that he discharged his rifle "fourteen times "—making once for every ten minutes that "the contest lasted." The others doubtless did as much; and such riflemen were accustomed to fire only with fatal aim. It is yet told, and well believed among their descendants, that these men "scarcely 'lost' a single ball in all that battle." With other light armed militia they were posted in the front lines, and commenced the action; but a panic seized the troops stationed as their support, and the Valley riflemen were left standing alone. Tradition tells that Capt. Tate, who commanded the Augusta company, mortified at the cowardice of the desertion, feigned not to hear the order then sent his company to retreat, and stood his ground fighting till himself and great numbers of his men fell dead upon the field, and Tarleton's resistless cavalry cut through their thinned ranks. The British General, Cornwallis, made special inquiry, after the battle, concerning "the rebel troops that were stationed in the apple orchard and fought so furiously;" and the American commander, General Greene, afterwards said to Maj. Alex. Stuart, of this Regiment, that there was a time in the fortunes of that day, when, if he could only have foreseen the unflinching bravery and fatal fire of these mountain riflemen, he would have annihilated the army of Cornwallis.

""

The memorable battle of King's Mountain was won by men of this same race; many of whom, like their gallant leaders—Campbell, Shelby and Sevier were born or reared in Augusta, tried in her forest conflicts, and conspicuous in the bloody battle of Point Pleasant. The "mountain men of North Carolina and Tennessee were of the same stock; and it is probable that all engaged in the action were immediate descendants of the Scotch-Irish Settlers. General Wm. Campbell, the chief commander, wore upon the field the same trusty sword his Grandfather bore in the Highlands of Scotland. The leading incidents of the battle are characteristic of the people themselves. When the news came that Ferguson and his formidable band were invading their mountain homes, their intrepid spirit was aroused to instant resistance. They awaited not to organize an equal army, and march in solid column against their formidable foe: nor needed they any baggage trains or camp equipage to delay and encumber their movement. Their tried rifles ever hung ready in their reach; their strong steeds were saddled at the word; the sound of the invader's approach was their call to the field, and their instinctive rallying place was the front of the foe. "All of a sudden," says a chronicler in Ferguson's army, "a numerous, fierce and unexpected enemy sprung up in the depths of the desert; the scattered inhabitants of the mountains assembled without noise or warning, daring, well mounted, and excellent horsemen." The numbers assembled reached two thousand, but lest the enemy should evade them, nine hundred of the best mounted pushed on—many of the officers in the ranks as private volunteers—and soon brought Ferguson to bay on that fatal mountain, "from which he boasted that all the rebels from hell could not drive him." But, in a short hour the haughty Briton and his army were surrounded and pressed in affright upwards to the mountain's crest; his men fell like leaves before the leaden hail; the fiery circle closed faster around him, and soon his own white horse came careering, riderless, down the mountain side, and his surviving troops threw down their arms in unconditional surrender. But now that the victory was won, the work of this impromptu and patriot army was over. The few words of the historian, Irving, truthfully tell the remainder of the characteristic story: "This victorious army of mountain men, did not follow up this signal blow. They had no plan of campaign; it was a spontaneous rising of the sons of the soil to revenge it on its invaders; and having effected their purpose, they returned in triumph to their homes."

And nearer our own homes tradition loves still to tell of another time when the "sons of the soil" rose in patriotic ardor to avenge it on the threatening invader. The dashing Tarleton, at the head of his "legion of devils," mounted on the swift race-horses, pillaged from the stables of the planters in Eastern Virginia, swept up the valley of James river and the Rivanna, made a descent upon Charlottesville, and into the very portals of Monticello, driving the Governor of this proud Commonwealth, a refugee, into the forests of Albemarle, and the Legislature in hasty flight across the mountains to Staunton, the frontier town of the State. Flushed by his successes, it was thought he would follow in pursuit and invade this mountain-girt valley, never as yet profaned by the foot of a foreign foe.

And on one quiet Saturday evening, when the rural inhabitants were resting from the labors of the week, and awaiting with accustomed reverence the holier rest of the coming Sabbath, an express rider came dashing across the mountain with the startling tidings that Tarleton was already approaching towards Rockfish Gap. The express passed on his way a house where religious service was holding, and one who was then present, and yet lives in a green old age, tells with faithful memory how the pious and patriotic pastor (Rev. Archibald Scott) at once, in thrilling tones, invoked his people to rally all their strength, and, with their lives in their hands, drive back the invader. The wives and daughters he hastened to their homes to help prepare their husbands, brothers and lovers for the defense of their firesides and their honor. By nightfall, the men mounted on what horses could be had, or on foot, were all moving towards the mountain gap, armed with their ready rifles, but some, for want of better weapons, carrying their mowing scythes and iron-forks, saying as they went, "we will 'turn our plough-shares into swords, and our pruning-hooks into spears,' to meet the invader of our land."

The alarm spread with the speed of the fiery cross along their ancestral highlands of ancient Scotland, and by early morning the whole valley was in motion, not as was their wont on that sacred day to gather in the houses of prayer, but in the familiar sentiment of their fathers, that "resistance to tyrants is obedience to God," they marched forth with the blessings and under the command of their patriot pastors, who, on that day, hesitated not to exchange the Bible and the pulpit for the sword and the saddle. And soon all along that misty mountain's top there bristled an armed host that might well have dismayed a stouter heart than Tarleton's. We may almost be forgiven the vanity of wishing that he had not been turned from the attempt, well believing, from the temper which rallied such a host, that the proud Tarleton would have met a resistance in that unconquerable spirit that courage never to submit or yield, which would have immortalized our own mountain pass with a victory memorable as that of the Swiss Morgarten, or if defeat, itself still glorious as that which forever hallows the ground where "the unconquered Spartans still are free, In their proud charnel of Thermopylae."

No wonder the immortal Washington, ever remembering the ready patriotism of the men of Augusta, who had stood by his side so valiantly on the fields of his youthful fame, and had won laurels for themselves in an hundred other battles, should have paid them the tribute of recommending their favorite leader, Andrew Lewis, for the commander-in-chief of the American armies. No wonder that in the darkest days of the patriot cause, when the bravest despaired, he still hopefully relied on the men of these mountains, and appointed the last refuge and rallying-place for freedom's followers among the fastnesses of Augusta. And no wonder that he has left the priceless legacy to them and their children's children forever, to found in their midst this noble Seminary of learning, a blessing to increase in every rolling year, a memento at once of his patriotism and wisdom to be cherished as long as his own immortal memory endures.

But if time permitted, it might well be shown that it was not only in arms they magnified and honored themselves and their country. When all for which they had taken the field was won, and the bugles sang truce at last, these unceasing worshippers at the shrine of liberty rested not until they had secured from the government of their own adoption all their long sought rights of religious as well as civil liberty. True to the sentiments inherited from the highlands of Scotland, and the shores of Ulster, they were still most ardent, and zealous and persistent advocates for a charter of religious freedom. The Presbytery of Hanover, having a large constituent proportion within this valley, moved in the matter as early as 1773, and again at Timber-ridge Church, in Rockbridge, in 1775, and presented an able memorial in 1776 to the General Assembly for the "removal of every species of religious as well as civil bondage." Again, in 1777, assembled at Timber-ridge, they earnestly "remonstrated against a general assessment for any religious purpose," declaring that its "consequences are so entirely subversive of religious liberty, that if they should occur in Virginia we should be reduced to the melancholy necessity of saying with the Apostles in like cases—'Judge ye whether it is best to obey God or man,'—and of acting as they acted." In 1780 another like memorial went up from Old Tinkling Spring, in Augusta; another in May, 1784, from Bethel, in Augusta; another in October, 1784, from Timber-ridge; and on the 10th of August, 1785, from a "General Convention at Bethel Church," in the midst of old Augusta, was started that famous petition to which 10,000 signatures were attached, and was finally instrumental in securing, on the

17th of December, 1785, the "inestimable statute for religious freedom" under which, in the prophetic words of the memorialists themselves, "civil and religious liberty go hand in hand, and our latest posterity will bless the wisdom and virtue of their fathers."

But the plan of this discourse concludes it where the worn channels of history so widen to the view. The incidents illustrating the characteristics of the settlers of this beautiful valley have been traced from the uncertain sources of the stream, arising far back in the sequestered retreats of tradition, until at length it has emerged on the more open tracts of Time, and rolls its deepening waters broad and clear in the sunlight of history.

The gleanings we have gathered may suffice, in some more skillful hand, to weave for their memory an enduring garland of glory. Enough may now have been given to illustrate their leading traits of activity of intellect, independence of spirit, fervency of patriotism, and perseverance of valor, and all adorned with a deep reverence for religion almost innate. These virtues may not have been adjusted in proportion, or polished into perfect harmony, but they were appropriate to the sphere of such simple life, and must command admiration for the solid strength and bold relief in which they stand, finishing upwards ever with the graces of piety and faith-like some old cathedral of the ruder ages, sublime for its very boldness of outline and massive strength of foundation, and pillar and wall, while gracefully from every loftiest part still springs the "taper spire that points to heaven."

For more than half a century these people were passing through troubles, through wars and rumors of wars; enduring cruel tortures on the heaths of Scotland, sore distresses in the fens of Ulster; terrors by day and night;

deadly struggles with savage foes in the forests of America, and resistance to the bitter end against the oppressions of England. Now they might well trust that their trials were ended, and find at last the peaceful sunset of their life radiant with the thought that their sufferings had not been in vain, but had won for their children that priceless blessing they so long had vainly sought—FREEDOM! and in its holiest sense, "FREEDOM OF THOUGHT, FREEDOM OF SOUL, salient, fathomless, and perennial spring of all other freedom."

The three-score years allotted to life had silvered the heads of the earliest settlers of this now peaceful valley, and like grain fully ripe, they were fast falling before the scythe of the relentless Reaper. But they had honestly filled up the full measure of life, and having fought a good fight, and finished the work given them to do, they could now lie down in the tomb as to peaceful sleep and pleasant dreams. Hallowed be their memories forever! The clods of the valley rest lightly on their graves—their forms "are dust; Their good swords rust; Their souls are with the Saints, we trust."

Well might lofty columns of marble be reared to honor their worth, and the pen of epic poet tell the story of their heroic lives. But at the least, let their memory be embalmed in the hearts of their descendants, and their examples be perpetuated in practice as faithfully as they received and transmitted them from honored sires in other lands; and let each and all again be invoked to strive with jealous and persistent effort to rescue something of their history from the fast gathering shades of oblivion, and so shall they contribute to rear them a monument more enduring than marble or brass. Indian tradition tells that "when a brave warrior had fallen, it became a sacred duty for each member of the tribe as he passed to throw a handful of earth upon the tomb; that thus they honored his memory from age to age, till by their pious tributes that tomb became the mighty mound upon our western plains." So let their descendants honor the memory of the brave settlers of this valley; so let the memory grow from age to age with increasing magnitude, till like that lofty mound upon the level prairie, it stands out green and beautiful against the horizon of time.

www.ingramcontent.com/pod-product-compliance
Lightning Source LLC
Chambersburg PA
CBHW051402280526
45784CB00007B/3068